FASHIONS OF A DECADE
THE 1950s

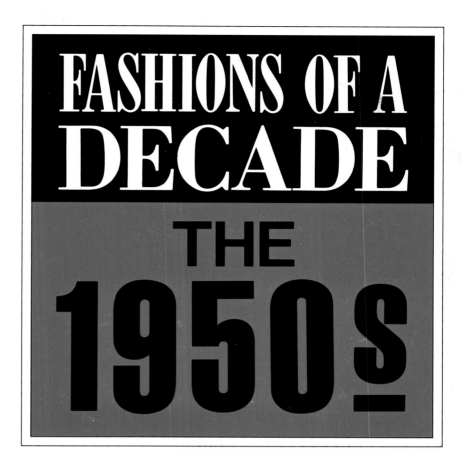

FASHIONS OF A DECADE

THE 1950s

Patricia Baker

**Series Editors: Valerie Cumming and
Elane Feldman
Original Illustrations by Robert Price**

B. T. Batsford · London

Contents

THE 1950s (FASHIONS OF A DECADE SERIES)

Text design by Sue Lacey
Jacket design by Sue Lacey
Composition by Latimer Trend & Company Ltd, Plymouth
Manufactured by Bookbuilders Ltd
Printed in Hong Kong
For the publishers:
B. T. Batsford Ltd
4 Fitzhardinge Street
London W1H 0AH

ISBN 0 7134\6639 1
A CIP catalogue record for this book
is available from the British Library.

THE 50S

January 1, 1950, was like any other New Year's Day. There was no change of direction on the political, economic (or fashion) scenes to mark the start of the new decade. The election of World War II hero Dwight Eisenhower as U.S. president in 1952 and in Britain the coronation in 1953 of Elizabeth II as

Queen were noted milestones in a decade when many looked back to the alliances and achievements of the Second World War as something solid to hold onto in a world newly split by East-West tension and the terrifying possibility of nuclear war. This conservative mood dominated the early years of the decade – whether in the

United States, which had emerged from the war years with increased prosperity, or in the European countries still rebuilding their shattered economies. This group certainly included the United Kingdom, where rationing and austerity continued into the new decade.

The Coronation of Queen Elizabeth II

Two years after she had square-danced her way into the hearts of many North Americans, wearing a circular felt skirt, Princess Elizabeth was crowned Queen. On June 2, 1953, donning a heavily embroidered ivory satin gown and train (designed by Norman Hartnell), she accepted the orb and sceptre at Westminster Abbey. For the first time, the coronation ceremony itself and the parades were seen by millions, thanks to television. In a Britain still bearing the scars of war, the coronation symbolized a new beginning. Mount Everest had just been scaled for the first time, most of the wartime rationing of food and clothing had been removed, building programs for homes, schools and hospitals were under way – it all seemed to point to the start of a New Elizabethan age, full of opportunities, discoveries, and prosperity, just as the accession in 1558 of Elizabeth I had.

It was different in the USA, where wartime restrictions had been quickly removed, and where the new "consumer society" was forging ahead – helped by new developments such as the start of the credit card system in 1950. But these differing conditions produced a similar effect on fashion both in Europe and America – a tendency to prefer the safe and normal, a veering away from the radical and extreme. "Normal" felt good, especially with the memory of the war still so fresh in many people's minds.

Bathing Belles. Swimsuits designed by Klein of Montreal.

The "exciting new colours" for the kitchen of the fifties were pastel, feminine shades, usually associated with bedroom or bathroom interiors.

Forest of Aerials

Suddenly television aerials were appearing on hundreds of roofs. By 1954 one person in every 24 in the United Kingdom had a TV set. Soon everyone was humming the commercial "jingles". Viewers on both sides of the Atlantic could watch the antics of Lucille Ball and Desi Arnez in the *I Love Lucy* show and the thrills of *Dragnet*. So different from the cosy British police series *Dixon of Dock Green*.

COMMUNIST PARTY ORGANIZATION U.S.A.-FEB. 9, 1950

Senator Joseph McCarthy shows the distribution of 250,000 Communist "fellow travellers" across the United States.

The world, however, *was* changing. A People's Republic had been established in China in 1949. India was enjoying the independence gained from Britain in 1947. The year 1952 symbolized a new beginning in Egypt, with the departure of King Farouk, while the death of Joseph Stalin in 1953 marked the end of an era for citizens of the Soviet Union. The Second World War had brought the end of the European colonial empires, and Third World countries were beginning their efforts toward economic development and political unity.

Although the war was over in one sense, the American government, the military and the general public were becoming increasingly apprehensive over the extent of Communist influence in Asia and at home. Communism had to be contained, whether in the rice paddies of Korea or in the film studios of Hollywood. In the last resort, it was thought, the nuclear bomb would stop the enemy, and during the decade there were a number of political crises when everyone thought the bomb just might be used. Slowly a realization of what this could mean began to spread and questioning of government and military policies began to gain ground, along with a cynicism among the young that was to be the hallmark of the 1960s.

The Appliance of Science

The notion that science could control nature (or even improve on it) had seized the public's imagination. Designs and patterns based on chemical or atomic structures on household products and furnishings, and chrome car-fins resembling rocket-jets, all show the fascination at all levels with science at this time. Whether it was in the field of nuclear energy or in the development of man-made substances (e.g. nylon and plastic) and electronics (e.g. computers), science promised to have the answer to every problem. All that the individual had to do was sit back and enjoy the fruits of

The McCarthy Hearings

Fears that Communists were attempting to undermine the American way of life – "Reds under the bed" – were widespread in the early fifties. U.S. senator Joseph McCarthy declared, but never substantiated his claims, that over 260 members of the State Department were Communist sympathizers or party members. A "witch-hunt" and smear campaign began, with McCarthy heading the Senate Investigations Sub-committee of 1953. The televised hearings lasted for over a month, but even after they had been wound up, the allegations continued, ruining many people's lives and careers. Between three and five million immigrants were said to be "subversive"; over 100 Hollywood film-studio personnel were denounced; 600 Protestant clergy were accused of being secret party members; and in 1957, over 700 organizations and publications were branded Communist agencies.

Elizabeth Eckford tries to attend Central High School in Little Rock, Arkansas, in April 1957.

Little Rock and Discrimination

Segregation in the American military and government services was officially ended in 1953, and one year later the Supereme Court ordered schools to integrate pupils, whatever their race, "with all deliberate speed". Many southern states resisted this ruling for as long as possible, with the governor of Arkansas in 1957 using National Guard troops to ensure that no black students entered Central High School in Little Rock. His action resulted in federal troops going in to open up the school to all students. By then, Dr Martin Luther King and others had initiated a number of boycotts against segregated buses, trains, parks, beaches, lunchcounters and diners.

hard work in the community and a contented family life. That was the theory. Life wasn't quite like this for everyone. Many saw migration as a route to a better life. A substantial number of Puerto Ricans left for America's mainland cities. Other peoples migrated from the Caribbean to Britain and France, introducing a substantial black population into these countries for the first time. Migration to Britain from India and Pakistan also began to gather pace. However, despite the bravery shown by members of non-white communities in the Second World War and later in Korea, racial discrimination was widespread.

Government responses to racial tensions were often hesistant and over-cautious, and increasingly the communities themselves began to take matters into their own hands – such as the Civil Rights movement in the USA. And while (for example) black cultures had made as yet little impact on main-stream fashion, seeds were being sown that would bear fruit in the coming decades.

ht Scene by Cleveland Museum of Art   *Lace Evening Gown by Hattie Carnegie*   *'56 Century—Four-Door Riviera—by*

Body by Fisher

Pioneers of today's newest and most thrilling advance in motorcar styli
the Four-Door Hardtop — as well as the wide-vision *Panoramic Winds*
and other famous Fisher Fashion Firsts found only on all GM cars for

CHEVROLET   PONTIAC   OLDSMOBILE   BUICK   CADIL

Individualist. Jacques Fath's stark
colours and simple, structured
shapes proved more popular in the
USA than in his native France.

Style often meant super luxury,
whether it was the use of lots of
shiny chrome or lace, shimmering
with sequins.

The Space Race

It seemed in the 1950s that science had answers to all problems. Nuclear power appeared to be a cheap, efficient and clean source of energy. The threat of a thermonuclear bomb could persuade hostile nations to meet for peace talks. The discovery of the structure of DNA (deoxyribonucleic acid), the molecule that carries the body's genes, paved the way for important medical research. However, the one scientific development to take hold of everyone's imagination was the first satellite in space. The successful Soviet firing of *Sputnik I* in October 1957 quickly followed by *Sputnik II* with Laika, a husky dog, aboard, shattered the confidence of Western nations, which had assumed they were ahead in science and technology. The space race was on. The first much-publicized attempt by the USA to put a satellite into orbit in December failed, but by February 1958 the American *Explorer I* was orbiting the earth.

The Young Ones

Pop records with titles like "White Sports Coat" and "Blue Suede Shoes" indicate the interest the young had in clothes but for the most part, young people (in the fifties, this meant 17–25 year olds) were expected to dress like their elders, according to their gender. Few retail outlets paid attention to them, although in the United States it was estimated that young people probably had $9 billion disposable income to play with (according to *Newsweek* in 1957). Women's magazines did tentatively raise the subject of young fashion but agreed that the difference in dress should lie in the accent ("less sophisticated") and not in styling.

Teddy Boys, 1955. Harmless enough to look at, but regarded by many as dangerously antisocial in the conformist climate of mid-fifties Britain.

So it was full skirts and stiff petticoats or, perhaps, a pencil-slim skirt and sweater with all the trimmings for girls. Tight-fitting pedal pushers or capri/pirate pants reaching to the calf were popular leisure wear and jeans (then called dungarees) were becoming acceptable with Marilyn Monroe and Princess Alexandra, both being photographed in them. For the young men it was shirt, tie and carefully pressed trousers, unless you were rebelling against your family and society in general, that is. Then you rejected this type of dress in favour of clothing that was darker in colour, rougher in texture, more crumpled in appearance or clearly exaggerated in styling. And people noticed.

One fad for girls in the USA was to wear a man's shirt outside their trousers. These would for preference be denims. In high school, a twin sweater set or Peter Pan-collared blouse were favoured looks. Dress-up events meant wearing special outfits.

Rock and roll star Little Richard: linen suit teamed with striped shirt and no tie – and T-shirt on display.

Elvis Presley

The phrase "Rock and Roll" was first heard in 1934 but was used in 1951 to describe a new type of American popular music that used elements of gospel, rhythm & blues, country and boogie. Five years later, Elvis Presley was its undisputed king, both in America and abroad, with such hits as "Blue Suede Shoes" and "All Shook Up." By today's standards his stage performances seem rather tame, but for many in the 1950s, they were outrageous, oozing with steamy masculine sexuality, so much so that when Elvis appeared on the popular Ed Sullivan TV show his hip gyrations were concealed from viewers.

For formal events – weddings or school proms American young women wore elaborate formal wear similar to that of their elders. But clothing choices were different for informal school dances. Widely popular in this period, many would take to the dance floors and jive to the infectious sounds of the hugely popular rock and roll rhythms. Also popular, but not quite as much, were the Latin rhythms of the cha-cha, mambo and merengue. Distinctive but informal clothing was the rule for these kind of dances. Many girls favoured very full skirts, some almost circular – particularly those made of wool felt fabric appliqued with bright motifs, including the widely seen poodle on a leash. These were worn with tight-fitting blouses tucked neatly into the skirt, and were often anchored with a very wide waist-cinching belt, and flat-heeled shoes.

A Man's World

As far as the family was concerned, the message pushed by the media was that the male was the bread-winner, returning home to relax and perhaps do a few household repairs. He had unquestioningly obeyed orders in the war; now he obeyed the commands of Big Business. He dressed in a dark, quiet, understated manner for the workplace but relaxed in slightly looser, more colourful clothing during leisure hours. As the decade progressed, his jacket got longer, the shoulders less padded and the trousers narrower in the leg (but just as perfectly pressed). The avail-ablility of new man-made fabrics did not mean any radical change in suit styling, just reduced weight of cloth and some experimentation in colour and texture in the weave.

Debbie Reynolds

James Dean stars in *Rebel Without A Cause.*

The Korean War (1950–53)

At the end of the Second World War, Korea was divided along the 38th parallel into North and South Korea, occupied by Soviet and American forces respectively until 1948. Two years later, North Korean troops crossed the border to invade the South, capturing Seoul in three days. Quickly the U.S. president, Harry Truman, sent American soldiers and called on the Allies for military assistance. After bitter fighting and great loss of life on all sides, the 38th parallel border was reestablished. However, this was not the end of American military action in the Far East. By the end of the decade the U.S. government became involved in suppressing Communist guerilla activities in South Vietnam.

However, a revolution was happening in the supply of clothing. Wartime garment production had resulted in increased efficiency, lower costs and standardization in quality and sizes. Already, mass-produced men's shirts were available from chainstores. No wonder bespoke, or custom-made, garments were speedily giving way to ready-to-wear clothes. As retail menswear outlets showed steadily climbing profits, British and French fashion designers sat up and took notice.

There were other changes. The demand for waistcoats was declining, while men's cardigans, as worn by film-star Rex Harrison, were slowly becoming acceptable at work. In Great Britain no gentlemen would be seen outside his family circle in braces, although the habit of wearing these was dying with the younger men increasingly relying on belts and zippers.

Hats too were losing popularity on both sides of the Atlantic, although they were featured frequently in advertisements and films. For the older generation, who still wore them, there were hat styles for every occasion, over 17 in fact. Most men preferred the safe and rather military "short back and sides" haircut, with a side parting, slicked back with haircream, but some young men were risking crew-cuts, or cultivating a quiff.

At first daytime leisure wear retained the rather military look with the fitted sports jacket or even a navy double-breasted blazer with ornate badge on the left breast pocket, worn with grey flannels or cavalry twill trousers. Increasingly though, during the decade, leisure wear began to mean a more colourful, open-necked sports shirt in drip-dry poplin, the comfortable sweater and slip-on shoes.

Fibres and Fabrics

The impact of the new artificial fabrics and fibres was really felt in underwear and leisurewear, although as early as 1952 haute couture designers, such as Christian Dior, Jacques Fath, Pierre Balmain and the House of Lanvin, were using them in their designs. It was the practical opportunities such fabrics offered – lightness but warmth, minimum shrinkage, quick-drying and waterproofing – that were exploited to the full extent in sportswear designed with an eye to both style and function. With men's and women's underwear, the impact was not so much in styling

(Opposite): The Wild One: Marlon Brando in jeans and leather jacket.

Hollywood's men in grey flannel suits: Cary Grant and James Mason star with Eve-Marie Saint in Alfred Hitchcock's 1959 thriller *North by Northwest*.

THE SATURDAY EVENING POST

NYLON
gives you something extra

Solid comfort under the Christmas tree! Men's easy-wearing nylon shorts and tops are a snap to wash and dry, need little or no ironing—new convenience for the Man Who Travels. How they wear!

Holiday sportsmen cheer for sturdy nylon ski jackets! They're comfortable—and they're light. They're tough to tear—and they take all the long, hard wear you give them winter after winter!

it all started with a stocking—and now—this Christmas—just look at all the wonderful things you can buy of nylon! Sheer pretties—and pretty practicals. Long-wearing lovelies—and lovely washables! For holiday giving—there's no end to the happy, easy-living parade of fashions in nylon!

Warm welcome for Santa Claus! Nylon nighties keep young ones cozy; keep their shapes, too, after a quick tubbing. Thrift note: they'll last through many a journey to the Land of Nod.

HAVE A MERRY CHRISTMAS—have a Christmas tree with lots of bright packages underneath—filled with welcome gifts of nylon—things to wear and use all year round!

There are lovely, lacy nylon bed jackets, tough nylon luggage, frilly—or softly tailored—nylon blouses, rugged nylon fishing lines; fluffy, warm nylon sweaters; tough, washable golf jackets.

Nylon gives you—at Christmas and the whole year round—strength; easy washing; fast drying; light weight; moth-, perspiration- and flame-resistance—and of course, nylon can be "heat-set" to hold its shape. Nylon Division, E. I. du Pont de Nemours & Co. (Inc.), Wilmington 98, Delaware.

DON'T STOP HERE! Homemakers, thrifty shoppers, club-women, students, write today for new free book, "Nylon Gives You Something Extra." **MANUFACTURERS:** send for "Nylon Textile Fibers in Industry." Nylon Division, E. I. du Pont de Nemours & Co. (Inc.), Wilmington 98, Delaware.

Du Pont makes only the nylon fibers—not the finished products shown here.

DU PONT
REG. U.S. PAT. OFF.

BETTER THINGS FOR BETTER LIVING
. . . THROUGH CHEMISTRY

FOR NYLON . . . FOR RAYON . . . FOR FIBERS TO COME . . . LOOK TO DU PONT

Nylon wasn't just for lingerie and stockings. It was beginning to be used extensively in men's underwear, socks and sportswear

Figure-hugging pants and shirt blouses were acceptable dress for women "entertaining the modern way". Postures and decor hint at artistic and even Bohemian life-st

From the Cool to Hard Bop

Pop music of the fifties had few intellectual pretensions, so if you were young and hip, your music had to be jazz – but which jazz? *Jazz on a Summer's Day*, the film of the 1957 Newport Jazz Festival, mirrors the quality and variety of the fifties jazz scene – from the vocal art of Anita O'Day and Dinah Washington to the avant-garde style of Chico Hamilton, and from the New Orleans trad of Louis Armstrong to the gospel of Mahalia Jackson and the sophisticated rock and roll of Chuck Berry. Elsewhere, Miles Davis was building on the reputation he established in the late forties with a series of stunning small and large ensemble recordings, working with the likes of Gil Evans, John Coltrane, Bill Evans and Cannonball Adderley. Art Blakey's Jazz Messengers were emphasizing the beat of the be-bop style (through Blakey's own explosive drumming) and coming up with the more soulful and even danceable "hard-bop" sound. And in the very last year of the decade, sax-man Ornette Coleman released the first of a series of revolutionary, atonal "free jazz" recordings that were to reverberate right through the next decade.

"You've taken me out every night," said Falloleen. "People wonder if maybe we're afraid to be alone with each other."

The Cold War and Khrushchev

The Communist takeover of Czechoslavakia in 1948, and also the blockade of the Western Allies' sections of Berlin did nothing to improve relations between Moscow and Washington. Even after Stalin's death in 1953, when control of Soviet affairs increasingly passed to Nikita Khrushchev, tension did not lessen. On the international stage Khrushchev alternated between the "good guy" and the "bad guy". Although, during his 10 years of power, he tried to improve living standards of the average Soviet citizen, massive resources went to build up Soviet military power. Diplomatic crises continued throughout the decade, caused by the sending of Soviet tanks into Hungary to suppress the National Rising in November 1956 and the attack by Britain and France on Egypt following its nationalization of the Suez Canal.

at this time – after all, this was governed by the shape of the outer garments – but in reduced weight, increased wearability and easier laundering. However used, man-made fibres had one other important effect and that was colour. With fabrics that could be washed and dried almost overnight without fear of shrinkage, there was no reason why light and pastel shades couldn't be worn even in the filthy smogs of London.

"Now you wash only your stockings." Scientists were not only working on satellites for outer space, but also on domestic chores such as laundry.

Woman, Wife and Mother

According to the media, a woman's place was firmly in the home, and particularly in the kitchen. Women's magazines proclaimed that "Femininity begins at Home." The best career was marriage and raising a family: to remain unmarried meant one was "emotionally incompetent". For many women who in wartime had enjoyed working outside the home and being in control of their own money, it was not an easy adjustment to make. By the end of the decade social commentators were noting the increased use of sedatives and anti-depressants and talking about the Trapped House-wife Syndrome.

Throughout the decade women's fashion, broadly based on Christian Dior's "New Look" of the late 1940s, promoted an idealized image of the happy housewife. The media continually used such adjectives as "soft", "charming", "feminine" to describe the clothing, yet most fashion photographic images show tall, slender, heavily corseted models, holding themselves in highly artificial, ballet-like poses, with little or no sign of emotion. No softness there. Few photographs showed the models in a work situation, outside or in the home.

Looking at fifties fashion illustrations for women, the relationship between waist and hips, and between neck and shoulders, becomes clear; both show the same emphasis and contrast. A figure eight is repeated from top to toe, and it was the same for garments from the fashion houses as from the discount stores. Until 1957, that is, when the loose-fitting styles of Hubert de Givenchy, Cristobal Balenciaga and Yves Saint Laurent for Dior heralded the new look of the 1960s.

For many, all this was far removed from reality. The fantasy of the Silver Screen was not only more attractive but perhaps more attainable. It was easier to identify with stars like Doris Day and Debbie Reynolds than with fashion models Bettina or Dorian Leigh. Even the sex symbols of the fifties were often photographed dressed like ordinary women, Brigette Bardot in gingham and Marilyn Monroe in jeans.

Film star Marilyn Monroe and playwright Arthur Miller: the marriage the media couldn't believe. Here Miller's conservative and formal male evening dress is a backdrop for Monroe's glamour.

Marilyn Monroe

She was *the* sex goddess of the decade. Signed up by 20th Century Fox in 1946, it was some eight years before Marilyn Monroe (formerly Norma Jean Baker) hit the big time with the film *Gentlemen Prefer Blondes* (released 1954), in which she worked alongside a sex symbol of the forties, Jane Russell. Although known for her figure, pouting mouth and wiggle (said to have been deliberately engineered by having high heels of different heights), Marilyn also had considerable acting talent, as seen in *Bus Stop*. Her marriage in 1958 to playwright and author Arthur Miller baffled the press, which could not imagine a love match between brains and beauty; the two qualities were surely incompatible.

Dream homes and dream families. Mother and father seem dressed for a big night out as soon as baby daughter is properly tucked up in bed.

"Handle with care." Cosmetics were seen as a sure-fire way of luring a man into marriage.

HANDLE WITH CARE...
IT'S LOADED WITH LOVELINESS!

NEW "pink T.N.T."

FABULOUS OFFER
"PINK T.N.T." SCARF

designed by Anne Fogarty

Get the lovely PINK T.N.T. scarf sho
here designed by Anne Fogarty! Impor
pure silk crepe; 35 inches square; hand-ro
edges! Guaranteed $3 value, it's yours
$1 plus tab or card marked Scarf Offer
PINK T.N.T. lipstick or polish. Mail w
name and address to Cutex, Box 110, N
46, N. Y. In Canada: Cutex, Box 1171, S
tion "O," St. Laurent, Montreal. Allow
weeks delivery. Expires Sept. 30, 1956.

Beautiful Dynamite for Lips and Fingertips

Gay as fireworks! Exciting as a carnival! "PINK T.N.T." is a radiant, rocketing new pink, sparked with a touch of blue. It's the hottest color that ever hit town . . . surefire ammunition for disarming your favorite masculine target! Get "PINK T.N.T." today and start the new season off with a beautiful bang!

NEW! CUTEX SATIN CLING LIPSTICK
Here's the new 24-hour-type lipstick by Cutex! Gives your lips round-the-clock color with no drying after-effect. 79¢. SHEER LANOLIN LIPSTICK, 59¢. For matching fingertips, chip-resistant CUTEX, longest wearing polish of all! Also, glamorous, iridescent PEARL CUTEX.

CUTEX
WORLD'S LARGEST SELLING MANICURE AIDS

22

Castro and Cuba

Fidel Castro, the lawyer son of a Cuban sugar planter, first attempted to overthrow the corrupt government of Cuba in 1953 but failed. After his release from prison, he fled to the United States and Mexico, returning secretly to the island in 1956 with about 80 supporters, including his brother Raul and Che Guevara. Moving from guerrilla tactics to public rejection of Fulgencio Batista's regime and all that it stood for, over a two-year period Castro became a popular leader, voicing the widespread discontent. His call for a general strike in April 1958 and the following disturbances finally forced President Batista to flee in January 1959. Castro became prime minister a month later.

High Fashion

Fashion itself was moving slowly from the catwalks of Paris, New York, Rome and London and select boutiques into the bigger shops and the multiple chainstores. The format of display "islands" as found in self-service supermarkets, with the message of low prices and high quality, was increasingly adopted in clothing shops.

The days of custom-made, or bespoke, tailoring were drawing to a close. Mass production techniques and processes, introduced in wartime to fill the bulk-clothing orders, were now going into action to supply the

new domestic demand; cutters could now handle 200 layers of cloth at one time. Faced with the growing importance of the ready-to-wear garment manufacturers, now offering standard sizes and all-around better quality, the fashion designers realized future success and indeed survival in changed postwar society now lay outside their traditional clientele.

They wanted both types of customer. So while quietly establishing commercial links with the mass garment suppliers and outlets in both America and Britain, the Paris fashion houses started down a highly publicized path of theatrical performance and selling the idea of "planned obsolescence", meaning that last season's wardrobe

Paris dictates. Dior 1955 – moving into the longer look and softer shoulderline.

The Suez Crisis

In the summer of 1956, worried by Egypt's increasing closeness with the Soviet Union and Eastern Europe, the United States and Britain withdrew their offer of financial help for the building of the Aswan Dam in Upper Egypt. As this project promised to transform the country's economic future, President Gamal Abdel Nasser reacted by immediately nationalizing the Suez Canal, explaining that canal dues would now go to finance the dam. The British and French governments – the major shareholders of the Suez Canal Company – began military attacks on Egypt that were widely and internationally condemned. The United Nations, backed by the USA and USSR, insisted on a cease-fire, and a peacekeeping force was sent in. Both British and French diplomatic reputations suffered, while Egypt and many other Arab countries increasingly looked to the Eastern bloc for support.

had to be thrown out, in favour of the new season's collection – a message repeated twice a year at the spring and autumn shows. To whet the public's appetite as well as to prevent their designs being copied immediately by mass-manufacturers, the fashion houses went to extreme lengths, banning any cameras and sketchbooks at the shows. Journalists and others feverishly attempted to beat the system, and their success or failure was avidly reported in the media, appearing almost more important than the actual collection.

Increasingly, the haute couture designs seemed far removed from the actual world, just as the models looked like untouchable goddesses. But for the moment, the clothing industry still paid attention to the major fashion shows, taking one or two features from the collections and incorporating them into their garments. Soon it was going to be the streets that set the pace in fashion.

Jaques Heim, 1956. For some, the New Look continued – in this case, with three-quarter length clutch coat, pearls and a full skirt with narrow waist.

Hardy Amies adopts another Dior creation – the S-Line. Note how the model's skirt has been pegged at the back to accentuate its cut.

(Following page): Twelve designers parade with their models – against a typically opulent background. These are the "big twelve" London designers, including Hardy Amies, Mattli, John Cavanagh and Victor Stiebel. The influence of Paris and Dior in particular can be clearly seen.

Living Dolls

Housewife Life

From the end of World War II, there was a concerted move to persuade women to leave their wartime jobs and return to looking after the family and the home. As leading American media adviser Ernst Dichter said: ''We helped the housewife rediscover that homemaking is more creative than to compete with men.'' However, by the end of the decade the *New York Times* and TV were talking of the ''trapped housewife''.

Yet the usual media image of a housewife showed her not as a mother in comfortable trousers and sweater, or loose dress, suitable for such work, but as a doll-like figure dressed in rustling, full skirts, nipped waist and narrow-fitting bodice. Even her apron had deep frills and a heart-shaped top and pockets.

The idea was that she should catch and keep her man, not by her personality and mind but by her young, slim, hour-glass appearance and long legs – all precariously supported on high stiletto heels.

One-piece bathing suits, strapless or halter-neck, boned and made from elasticated fabric, were more fashionable and popular than bikinis.

Living Doll. James Stewart begins the transformation of co-star Kim Novak into the exact likeness of the lost lover he believes to be dead, in Alfred Hitchcock's classic film *Vertigo.*

Working Women

If the role model for the housewife was the Girl Next Door, then Grace Kelly was the perfect role model for the working woman. A trip to town called for a trim, closely fitting suit — like the uniform of airline stewardesses — worn with high-heeled shoes. But there was little of eighties and nineties Power Dressing in this outfit. Everything hinted at fragility, whether it was the sloping shoulder line, the tailoring accenting the curve of the bust, rib cage, hip and pelvis, the heels emphasizing the ankle and calf, or the little hat with face-veil and feathers, gloves and small handbag.

Social life still retained some formality. For the more mature woman, theatre-going and even entertaining at home called for cocktail (ballerina length) and evening wear (floor-length). For young and old alike this meant the romanticized image of the swan-necked, soft-shouldered female in rustling taffeta, shimmering silks (real or artificial), or layers of pastel nylon net decorated with lace, ribbons and sequins.

New Styles in New Fabrics

The new man-made fabrics resulted in exciting developments in sportswear, where both fashion and function were equally important. American and Italian designers showed the way. Lightweight, but warm and easily cleaned sailing and ski jackets, based on wartime flying jackets, were now possible, with nylon as both padding and main fabric; zips eliminated drafty openings. Two-way stretch fabrics were quickly exploited for ski pants and motor-scooter slacks, with instep straps to produce a long, smooth tapered legline, and zips at the side (front zips were thought too provocative).

Swimwear also took advantage of man-made fibres. Elasticized two-way stretch fabrics were employed in figure-controlling one-piece suits, strapless or halter tops, with preformed or padded cups to guarantee the best projection. These suits, frequently styled on Esther Williams's bathing costumes, were worn with extravagant bathing caps. The more daring two-piece bikini, launched by the Parisian designer Louis Reard in 1946 after the atomic bomb test on Bikini Atoll, was gradually catching on — especially after British film star Diana Dors appeared in her mink version at the Cannes Film Festival. In America there was another choice: the revolutionary softly draped stretch jersey suits of Claire McCardell, who continued to design simple but stylish easy-to-wear coordinates.

Colour was everywhere, from the ski slope to the beach, with Italian designer Emilio Pucci in the forefront of the European leisurewear. His loose-fitting, printed-silk "scarf" blouses quickly became popular for holiday wear, while American women relaxed in tropic-patterned Hawaiian shirts and Bermuda shorts.

A fifties face. Bright red lipstick, liquid eyeliner emphasizing the eyes and pencilled eyebrows, with a peaches-and-cream complexion: all set off by a neat hat, pearlized stud earrings (pierced ears were unfashionable) and a white pique collar.

The late forties New Look of Christian Dior could still be seen in fashion throughout the fifties for shirtwaists or skirt and blouse, both with full skirts and slim-fitting bodices.

Colourful prints on a white background were summer favourites, as well as pastel floral motifs, but the tight-fitting bodices and narrow waists made no concessions to high temperatures.

The ideal fifties woman was a homemaker, bringing up her daughter to yearn for domesticity.

Two or more "can-can" petticoats of nylon, usually with frills of nylon net in pastel colours, were worn under full skirts. These were often stiffened by dipping in sugar solution and then drip-drying.

Man in the Grey Flannel Suit

Corporation Man

The fifties man was in demand at work, helping rebuild the economy, and also on the social scene. War had proved his bravery, endurance and ability to obey orders. It was his turn after a day's work to be waited upon by his wife, the homemaker. He didn't have to be fashionable: that was for the female. As the dependable bread-winner, his style of dress reflected the image of a clean-cut, white collar company man; sober, mature and anonymous.

This was the "Man in the Grey Flannel Suit", the subject and title of a 1955 novel by Sloan Wilson. Such men could be seen by their thousands going to work every weekday morning, all dressed in their "uniform" of a suit (usually single-breasted), white shirt, silk tie and carrying a brief case. Several fifties films played on the idea of the Man in the Grey Flannel Suit, besides the one based on Wilson's novel, which starred Gregory Peck. In Alfred Hitchcock's *North by Northwest,* Cary Grant stars as a Madison Avenue advertising man accidentally caught up in the world of Cold War espionage due to a case of mistaken identity.

Pierre Cardin was one of the first French designers to create a fashion range for men. These three high-button styles were shown in February 1950: (left) *Montparnasse à la Flannel* town suit with a Nehru collar; (center) *Saint Tropez* summer suit of striped cotton, complete with a furled umbrella; (right) *Toile,* a town suit.

"Have you met our distinguished guest?" remarks the chief villain on capturing the hero. "He's certainly a well-tailored one," replies an accomplice. Later, still attired in his grey flannel suit but now on the run from the law as well as the villains, Grant meets heroine Eve-Marie Saint on the Twentieth-Century Express to Chicago. "You know so little about me", he quips. "I know you've got good taste in food, good taste in clothes . . ." she replies. What more need be said? After a hair-raising adventure with a crop-duster armed with a machine gun, Grant gets his suit dry-cleaned before confronting the villains at an auction room and finally escaping death on the face of Mount Rushmore. He overcomes it all – and without changing his executive suit.

Ivy Leaguers

The grey flannel suit had also long been a favourite among the college men of the long-established East Coast universities, the Ivy Leaguers. The 1950s version was usually charcoal grey with a two- or three-button (widely spaced), single breasted jacket with narrow shoulders, long and unwaisted with one or no back vent; it was said to conceal the bulkier form of the American man. The English jacket was shorter and more fitted, usually with two back vents. By the mid-fifties the softer "Continental" shape popular on the West Coast of America and in Europe emphasized a slimmer, longer line, from lapel and shoulder widths down to the more tapered trouser leg, now without the turn-up.

The introduction of man-made fibres into men's suiting started American experiments in textures and colour. In 1951–52 there was a fashion for slubs – materials with "random" scattering of bright specks – and by 1955–56, synthetic silk-like suiting was popular, especially for the hotter months. Synthetic shirting meant shirts could be washed and drip-dried overnight. The shape of the collar was softening from long points, stiffened by celluloid tabs and moving into a shallow, rounded shape, associated with the Ivy League style, with a screw pin or fabric tab placed behind the tie-knot or else buttoned down to the shirt front.

Another part of Ivy League dress was the penny loafer. This was a comfortable slip-on, lace-less shoe, with a strip or "apron" across the front and tongue. The name "penny loafer" came from the idea of sticking a shiny cent behind the decorated cut-out shape of the apron.

Leisure Time

The one area where the American male displayed his individuality was in leisure wear. Matching plaid or contrasting beachwear sets of boxer shorts or elastic-waisted trunks with short-sleeved, loose-fitting cotton shirts or tops, worn open necked, were becoming commonplace. More colourful still were Hawaiian shirts and Bermuda shorts, which even the older man, like presidents Truman and Eisenhower, would wear. War service in the Pacific and Hawaii's final entry into the Union (in 1959) guaranteed the popularity of the vividly colourful shirt, but another reason was the featuring of such Hawaiian shirts in the successful film *From Here to Eternity* (1954), starring Montgomery Clift.

Invasion of the Body Snatchers. **Kevin McCarthy (left) thwarts an invasion from outer space in his grey flannel suit.**

Lounge suits were now acceptable dress not only for work but for many social occasions, providing the trousers had knife creases, the jacket fell well, and the shirt cuffs were just visible under the sleeve-cuffs. Man-made fibres meant that the weight of the suits could be reduced by almost half.

By the summer of 1957, jackets were longer and the line emphasized by softer shoulder padding and slim-cut lapels. But even for leisure hours, the British male had carefully pressed trousers. Hepworth, which was to link up with the designer Hardy Amies, was one retail outlet to take advantage of mass production.

American men were more adventurous when choosing textured weaves for leisure suits, but the four-button sleeve-cuff and two-button, narrow-lapelled jacket style echoes that of business suits.

American males led the way in enjoying the freedom of leisure wear, both in the loose fit and the vivid prints of sports shirts.

An Artificial Freedom

Laundry Trouble

The media continually exhorted women to "wash whiter" as part of their wifely and motherly duty. Commercial laundries and dry-cleaning shops weren't cheap and, anyway, water-resistant finishes on garments were removed during dry-cleaning until new processes were introduced in 1959. Laundrettes were still few and far between, so once a week the boiler, wash-board and heavy mangle would be dragged out, or – if you were lucky enough to own one – the lumbering top-loader washing machine with integral mangle would be pressed into service.

Suddenly, artificial fabrics came to the rescue. A number of them had been known for some time but only in the 1950s was there large-scale production, so dramatically increasing supply and lowering costs.

Nylon Revolution

Nylon – a by-product of petroleum originating from the Du Pont company in the 1930s – was first used for women's stockings and lingerie but with the war most output went to supply military needs for parachutes, ropes and tyres.

American manufacturers were released from wartime restrictions shortly after peace was declared, but British producers had to wait until the total end of clothes rationing in 1952.

The immediate demand was for nylon stockings, so much so that the word "nylons" quickly came to mean "stockings". But the advantages of nylon for underwear were considerable. Its easy-washing, shrink-proof and quick-drying properties along with its lightweight, hard-wearing qualities were all promoted: "Goodbye to mending" was the message. Nylon could be produced in all weights of fabric, from heavy fake fun-furs to the sheerest of lingerie. It could feel as soft as silk and yet be stiff enough to hold out the circular skirts of the dance dress.

Rayon and Beyond

Rayon was another low-cost, man-made fibre with a long history and a romantic luxurious aura as the name it was known by, "artificial silk" or "art-silk", suggested. Few women realized it was made from wood-pulp, with caustic soda for viscose and with cotton fibres and acetic acid for acetate.

By 1954 a by-product from petro-chemicals, Terylene, or Dacron as it was first known in the United States, hit the headlines. A polyester fibre, it had first been developed in Great Britain before the war but then taken up by the American company Du Pont. Like nylon it was easily washed, quick-drying and shrink-proof, as salesmen in America showed by diving into swimming pools or standing under showers fully clothed. It was also crease resistant, but able to take permanent pleating, which removed at a stroke the tiresome chore of ironing. Lightweight but warm, a man's suit made out of Terylene/Dacron weighed only 12 ounces rather than the usual 20, a boon in summer weather.

Suddenly there was no real reason why clothes should be in dark or sombre colours. Washing and drying could be done virtually overnight, rather than hanging around drying for days. Shrinkage, moth damage (real problems in the past for knitwear) and ironing were all virtually banished. All this could have given women more leisure time, but in fact surveys at the end of the decade showed they were spending 10 percent more time on household chores.

The polyester fibre Dacron (or Terylene, as it was known in Britain) became widely available after 1954 but led to no revolution in menswear styling. Belts rather than braces were used and a closer fit without waist pleats was preferred, even for leisure wear.

re neater ... **more comfortable**
with less care, outdoors or in, when you wear
slacks made with high percentages of "Dacron"* polyester
ey keep you neat-looking longer with less trouble, even in
eather, because "Dacron" holds off wrinkles while it holds
press. Cool slacks of "Dacron" are rugged, too, give you
ally long wear. See them in a variety of fabrics, styles, and
erever you buy your better clothes.

DACRON

REG. U. S. PAT. OFF.

DU PONT
REG. U. S. PAT. OFF.

BETTER THINGS FOR BETTER LIVING
...*THROUGH CHEMISTRY*

A fashion for Baby Doll nightwear, made from nylon or Tricel, followed the 1956 film of that name, starring Carroll Baker.

Pastel shades and accordion pleats were one of the most popular choices in the mid-fifties, thanks to man-made fibres.

The easy-to-care qualities of Orlon made it popular, particularly in knitwear.

Nylon stockings teamed with nylon lingerie.

iracle
time

iraculous fibres
is Orlon,* and
sweaters are
re, color and
ability. They
ke softness.
and vibrant,
ues that set the
ts and business.
no shrinking, no
fading—and the
rs are locked-in!
resistant, too.
red, at most
ne stores.

*ole Fibre

Robert Bruce
ORLON SWEATERS

E INC. • 159 W. ALLEGHENY AVENUE • PHILADELPHIA 33, PA

Haute Couture Heyday

Fashion Dreams from Dior

It was clear at the beginning of the decade that the fashion houses of the United States had failed to break the French designers' hold on haute couture. It was the catwalks of Paris that were prominently featured twice yearly in the glossy and popular magazines of the fifties. Yet, it was the American designers who responded more directly to the needs of the contemporary woman.

The biggest showman of all was Christian Dior. He grabbed the headlines time and again, right up to his death in 1957. Dior promoted dreams. When his "New Look" was first shown in 1947, he remarked that "fashion comes from a dream, and the dream is an escape from reality." Dior also introduced the idea of planned obsolescence, stating that "Novelty is the very essence of the fashion trade." A new collection emerged from the House of Dior every six months, and with each spring and autumn collection, new "lines" were announced, such as the Oval Line, Princess Line, Sinuous Line, and Profile Line (1952), H Line (1954), A line (1955), and the Trapeze Line (1958, the brainchild of Yves Saint Laurent). Other fashion houses had little alternative but to follow.

However, many fashion commentators believe that Cristobal Balenciaga was the designer who broke new ground. Spanish born, he was one of the few *haute couturiers* in Paris who knew how to cut: a master of technique as well as creativity. The tortoiseshell-like jacket back, 3/4 sleeves, slit vertical side pockets in skirts, and patch pockets showing below the suit jacket – all these are said to be his innovations. Well before Dior's 1954 H Line, Balenciaga was releasing women from the highly artificial hourglass shape and adopting a more fluid functional shape while retaining the accepted "romantic" image for evening wear. This looser style was then further developed by his close associate, Givenchy, with his famous chemise, or sack dress, of 1957, which was in turn taken up and exploited to great effect by Mary Quant and others in the early sixties.

The Givenchy sack took New York by storm, with American *Vogue* declaring in September 1957 that it was "More than a fashion, it's actually a way of dressing." In Britain Anita Loos argued in *Vogue* that the loose fit of the sack lent mystery to the wearer. "I mean, no gentleman is ever going to puzzle his brain over the form of a girl in a Bikini bathing suit."

Unmistakably Chanel

Coco Chanel was the one Paris designer who did design wearable clothes for women, rather than create an image that bore little resemblance to the demands of real life. She re-opened her fashion house in February 1954 but the show got mixed reviews.

The Chanel look was unmistakable, the straight skirt with or without box pleats, and the single-breasted cardigan jacket, with or without lapels, and

Christian Dior with models wearing some of his evening dress designs in April 1950.

with braid or ribbon trims of contrasting colour on the edges, hems, cuffs, and pockets, and teamed with a blouse with a pussycat bow. Chanel had argued "Fashion fades; only style remains the same", and her style was based on ease, comfort for the wearer and practicality.

American Innovation

American designers who had come into the limelight in the 1940s – like Norman Norell, James Galanos, Adrian – still remained influential.

Mainbocher, so important during the war years, continued with his accent on hips and waist, with fitted waist-length jackets and pencil skirts starring in his 1953 collection. Mainbocher was also responsible for starting the craze for beaded evening sweaters, and clearly he enjoyed himself designing costumes for movies such as *Call Me Madam* (1950) and *Wonderful Town* (1953). However, it was the easy, relaxed look of Claire McCardell's day and leisure designs in jersey, denim and cottons that

was to have the greatest and longest impact on American fashion, influencing Bill Blass and Calvin Klein. Bonnie Cashin also responded to the needs of the fifties woman by bringing fashion and style into separates – a wartime invention to get round clothing scarcities – and so firmly establishing the idea of mix-and-match coordinates for the following decades.

A, S and H lines: the three Paris silhouettes for autumn 1954.

"Will the ladies obey Monsieur Dior?"

Balenciaga coat, 1953. Loose, ample coats with interesting collars, made from textured fabrics (often mohair in the late fifties), provided a striking contrast to the close-fitting dress or suit worn underneath.

(Opposite): Balenciaga late-day dress of black tissue taffeta, Autumn 1951. An important feature was the sash either at the front or the back, drawing attention to the narrow waist and exaggerated hip curve.

Barbara Goalen wearing a 1953 Mattli "Petunia" evening dress. The extended shoulder detail emphasizes the pinched waist but echoes the wide ballerina-length skirt.

The Undercover Story

Corsets and Curves

The unstated message of the decade was that to catch and keep a man, female curves were all important. As the proper career for any young woman in the fifties was marriage and child-rearing, she had to show she was potentially good material for just that.

The line until the last years of the decade was smooth and soft, following the form of an hourglass or a figure eight – and so close-fitting that it looked almost like a second skin. All this perched on pencil-thin high heels. To achieve this look, the body had to be squeezed and imprisoned in stiffly boned corsetry. Dior may well have announced that he was ending the encasing of women in iron, but his dresses could literally stand up under their own devices, supported by their internal boned structures.

If France was seen as the home of the fashion designer, America was seen as the source of the perfect corset. Many shop-assistants studied for corsetry qualifications, as customers would frequently ask for a personal fitting, while news of a "revolutionary" design in stock could result in the shop being besieged by thousands of women. Fanciful, frothy names such as "Romance," "Merry Widow" and "Pink Champagne" were given to these cages that crammed the body into the desired shape. Gradually whalebone and steel stiffeners were replaced with lighter and less rigid plastic and celluloid "bones" and the introduction of zips meant much easier fastening. But what a relief to take off the foundation garment each evening.

Engineered for Uplift

Brassieres, short or long-line, called "Lovable" and "Sweet and Low", were similarly wired, particularly for the strapless and backless summer and evening dresses. The cups were padded and fully stitched to give the required shape and cleavage, while the advertising copy used architectural terms like "uplift" and "cantilevered comfort". One widely advertised brand promoted the idea that its brassieres were such an integral part of dress that the customer would forget to put on the actual top-garment, even to cross the road or to go to the theatre.

This design in corsetry promises "excellent abdominal support" from its "comfortable but firmly-boned construction".

Heels and Hose

The final part of the armour was the stiletto heel. If the pencil-slim and full skirts emphasised the fragile hourglass figure, the stiletto drew attention to the shape of the ankle and calf, and the movement of the hips in walking. Jourdan of Paris was the first to combine steel with wood for heels in 1951, but the Italian shoe designer Ferragamo is usually credited with the invention of the steel support in a synthetic heel that allowed a very small heel-tip. The impact was tre-

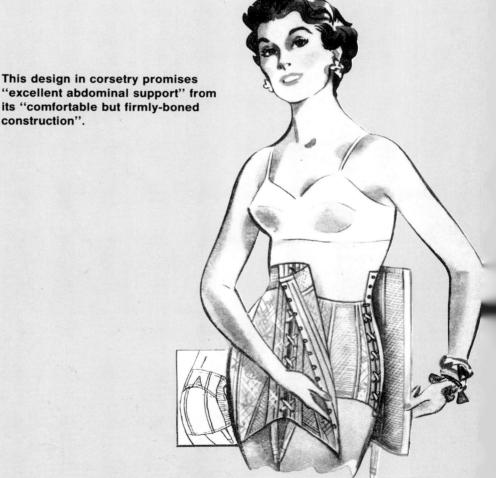

mendous, especially on floors. Airline management and hoteliers met hurriedly to discuss how to make floors impervious to the myriad of indentations suddenly appearing.

By 1958 the height of the heel had increased and the toe had become sharply pointed, the design of Beth Levine two years earlier, some say. Problems with posture and feet grew, and analogies with traditional Chinese foot-binding were drawn. However, many young women warded off unwelcome attention by "accidentally" bringing a heel down on an unsuspecting male foot.

By this time nylon stockings were not only finer and far cheaper but they had a much better shape. Perhaps it was this closer fit that encouraged designers to raise dress hems from the lower calf in 1952 to an inch or so above the knee by 1958. With this shorter length came the "bare-legged" look of seamless nylons.

The lifting of post-war restrictions resulted in an explosion of interest in cosmetics, encouraged by movie make-up artists entering the market. Cheeks were gently rouged, while eyes were emphasised by liquid eyeliners, a little eyeshadow and masses of mascara. However, it was the lips, women were told, that trapped the man, and most lipstick names implied cool seduction (into marriage, of course).

The face was framed by curls and gentle waves, carefully and painstakingly pinned up or pinched in clips before drying. Straight hair was definitely unfashionable, except when twisted back into a chignon or French pleat, but permanent waves, applied in the hair salon or at home, solved the problem of curls.

Halter-neck and strapless dresses with tight-fitting bodices required long-line strapless bras, which were wired and padded.

Pots, rather than bottles, of cosmetics decorated the dressing table, but loose powder and rouge were gradually being replaced by pan-sticks, developed from film and theatre make-up.

An exception to the heavily girdled and corsetted look were the designs of Claire McCardell, famous for her casual jersey (as shown in this 1950 swimsuit) and denim garments.

Even Cleopatra needs her bra . . .

I dreamed I played Cleopatra in my maidenform bra

The aim: an hour-glass shape to go with Dior's corsetted, wasp-waist look of 1950.

Hollywood Dreams

The Silver Screen

Fewer people were going to the movies than immediately after the war, preferring to stay at home watching television, listening to the radio or the record player, but for many, the weekly visit to the local cinema was still important. On the silver screen character stereotyping and lavish productions were the order of the day, with little of the experimentation found in some theatre productions. No-one, argued Hollywood, wanted reality; the customer preferred pure escapism, thrills, spills and happiness everafter – and a role model.

Girl Next Door/Boy Next Door

The Girl Next Door look was epitomized by Doris Day and Debbie Reynolds. The All-American Girl was squeaky clean, tidy and bubbling with health in a full skirt, wide tight belt and fitted blouse with a perky collar, white ankle socks and penny loafers or saddle shoes, with her hair in a ponytail. The Boy Next Door (also about 20 years old) was actually to be found on the college campus, wearing over his shirt a long cardigan or sports jacket and belted slacks or chinos (braces were definitely out). On his feet were easy-fitting penny loafers or white buckskin laced shoes, as popularized by Pat Boone. A bookish look and serious gaze, even horn-rimmed glasses, hinted at a certain vulnerability, which appealed to all ages of female film-goers. Perhaps, like Clark Kent, he might be transformed into Superman.

How the West Was Won

Throughout the 1950s westerns were very popular. These tales of ruggedly handsome good guys and sullen-faced bad guys, of action and romance offered welcome escape for the grey-suited businessman and confirmed the homemaking role of the fifties woman – as even the independently minded film heroine would surrender thankfully into protective masculine arms in the final scene. No wonder many American men in their leisure hours shed their tailored jackets and trousers for fringed suede jackets, plaid shirts, jeans worn with moccasins or cowboy boots, like their cinema heroes. As for women, the message was clear in *Calamity Jane*, in which Doris Day only got her man when she changed her masculine cowboy clothing for gingham dresses. Calico, homespuns, lace and crochet work similarly became popular with the dress-style based on Dior's New Look – but then that itself was rather mid-19th century in concept. The young American child also found a hero, Davy Crockett, subject of the 1955 Walt Disney film that netted $300 million from the spin-off products, more than from box-office receipts.

Shirley Jones as the Girl Next Door in *April Love* (1958). Women's trousers usually had side fastenings, as front zips for women were thought to be "naughty".

Cool and Sophisticated

This was the image that every woman really yearned to achieve, while elbow deep in the Monday washing suds. It spoke of good breeding, a comfortable income, sophisticated friends and a household of servants. Stars like Margaret Lockwood, Deborah Kerr, Kay Kendall, Grace Kelly and Kim Novak were the walking, talking versions of the haughty, elegant models who graced the runways of the Parisian fashion houses, but on the silver screen these stars seem to descend into the "real" world. Perhaps, just perhaps, given the money and opportunity, one could be like them . . .

Cool and Sophisticated

This was the image that every woman really yearned to achieve, while elbow deep in the Monday washing suds. It spoke of good breeding, a comfortable income, sophisticated friends and a household of servants. Stars like Margaret Lockwood, Deborah Kerr, Kay Kendall, Grace Kelly and Kim Novak were the walking, talking versions of the haughty, elegant models who graced the runways of the Parisian fashion houses, but on the silver screen these stars seem to descend into the "real" world. Perhaps, just perhaps, given the money and opportunity, one could be like them . . .

The Homewreaker

The pin-up girl of the forties was still a potent image in the fifties. The model was Jane Russell, one of the original "Sweater Girls" of the forties, famous for her bosom and bee-stung lips. She was the girl you *didn't* take home to meet mother. Her wardrobe was a mixture of the Girl Next Door and haute couture but more sexually inviting — a lower neckline perhaps, or a more close-fitting dress — she was no ice-cool goddess.

Equally famous were the cleavage of Elizabeth Taylor or Jayne Mansfield, the legs of Cyd Charisse, the wiggle of Marilyn Monroe. Continental films cultivated a more aggressive, earthy image, and with it, a younger focus. So from the female tiger role as played by Silvano Mangano in the Italian film *Bitter Rice*, there developed the Sex Kitten, made famous by the newly discovered French star Brigitte Bardot (*And God Created Woman*, 1956) and America's Carroll Baker (*Baby Doll*, 1956). Bardot's appearance in a gingham bikini in 1956 and her gingham wedding dress in 1959 and Baker's scanty, short pajamas in the film immediately sparked off demands for similar styles in stores and shopping malls.

The mid-forties look of Thelma Ritter's dress and shoes contrast with the mid-fifties style of Grace Kelly in a film still from Alfred Hitchcock's *Rear Window* (1954).

Carroll Baker in *Baby Doll* (1956) portrayed a mixture of sex-kitten and teenage Lolita.

For many film fans in the 1950s, Pat Boone was the personification of the clean-cut Ivy Leaguer – an All-American Boy Next Door with button-down collar and plain blue jacket.

Jane Russell in a classic sex goddess pose. More elegant sequined versions of the sheath dress were the hallmark of American designer Norman Norrell.

This Givenchy dress of 1955 features a mid-fifties narrow "pencil" skirt.

High Society. Bing Crosby, Grace Kelly and Frank Sinatra as depicted on the record jacket of the movie musical's soundtrack. Fifties Hollywood at its most lavish.

Cafe Society

Crazy World

Not everyone in the fifties wanted to be associated with a Gray Flannel Suit and a Living Doll image. The new decade had promised so much – the Second World War had been the "war to end all wars" or so one was told. But instead as the decade progressed the promises seemed to fade, with new political and military conflicts breaking out around the globe. It seemed that nuclear armaments might be used at any moment.

Relations between the West and the Eastern bloc were rapidly deteriorating and in America, Senator McCarthy's witch-hunts for so-called Communist sympathizers spread across all intellectual and cultural activities. The horizons of many young people were being widened through educational reforms, and on both sides of the Atlantic, the problem of racial discrimination could no longer be ignored.

"Where Go? What Do? What For?"

The nonconformists of the 1950s were the Beatniks, whose philosophy was summed up in these three questions put by beat poet and novelist Jack Kerouac in 1958. Journalists first suggested in 1952, when the movement took off, that "beat" stood for weariness ("dead-beat"), but Kerouac corrected them, saying his was "basically a religious generation" and "beat means beatitude, not beat up."

There were similarities with the postwar existentialist movement, when students and intellectuals had met in Parisian bistros to talk and argue over the latest writing of Albert Camus, Jean-Paul Sartre and Simone de Beauvoir. From America's West Coast, ideas spread to New York, and Greenwich Village in particular, and Allen Ginsberg's protest poem *Howl* could also be heard as far afield as the jazz-clubs and coffee bars of London.

Disquiet over established values was reflected in dress. The message was definitely antifashion and antiestablishment. The clean-shaven look and the neat hairstyle for men were out. So was the immaculately pressed gray flannel suit. Instead a turtle- or polo-neck sweater (preferably black in color), or crumpled shirt and unpressed trousers, khaki pants or jeans were worn. As for the young Beatnik woman, she dressed just as casually, in a black leotard, or perhaps a long, heavy "Sloppy Joe" sweater over a long black skirt worn with black tights. Occasionally she wore tight-fitting straight leg corduroy pants, but always flat-heeled ballet pumps on her feet. Black was the color for the Beatniks.

Miles Davis, Art Blakey, Thelonius Monk, Ray Charles, Milt Jackson and Ornette Coleman demonstrate different interpretations of jazz style from a selection of late-fifties record jackets.

One Cappuccino Please?

The focal point of all the activity was the coffeehouse – the favorite meeting place for Beatniks and would-be Beatniks in the early fifties. Here one could listen to play or poetry readings and "cool" music whether from the juke box, a jazz band or, in Britain, perhaps also the local Skiffle group, with their curious combination of folk music and rock and roll. But mainly it was here that one could just hang out, lingering over a cup of cappucino or expresso.

The impact of Italy was not just confined to the import of Gaggia espresso machines and Italian pop songs like "Che sera, sera" and "Volare." It was in leisure wear that Europe and Italy in particular was rapidly gaining an international name.

From 1950 both Lambretta and Vespa, Italian motor scooter manufacturers, aimed their sales promotion at the European youth market, stressing freedom of the roads, friendship and cheapness. It quickly became the "in" mode of transport throughout Western Europe, not only did it emancipate young Italian women but revolutionized their dress. Tight calf-length "capri" or pirate pants (also known as pedal pushers), or shorts were worn instead of full skirts, which could get caught in the wheels. Slipper or flat ballet shoes were best for motor scooter riding, while a turtleneck sweater or neckerchief prevented draughts down the neck. Striped knit tops with dolman sleeves lent a Continental air, and gave freedom of movement. Hair was styled in a short gamine cut or kept in place with a head-scarf.

The looser, longer "Sloppy Joe" sweaters of the late fifties worn with tight pants and flat shoes and glass or plastic Poppet beads.

A still from the movie of Jack Kerouac's sensational novel *The Subterraneans.* The movie was released in 1959.

The Italian pedal-pusher style for scooter enthusiasts.

Brigitte Bardot, a movie star for the Beats.

Rebels Without a Cause

Antiheroes?

There were those who wanted to sit and talk about the state of the world and there were those who broke from the established conventions by less intellectual methods. On the political scene, America's General Douglas MacArthur and Senator Joe McCarthy had won many supporters when they argued that action and retribution were better policies than diplomacy and compromise. On both sides of the Atlantic violence and sudden death featured in numerous films about World War II exploits, detective novels concerning the adventures of lone-wolf private investigators (like Mickey Spillane), and TV police series such as *Dragnet*. It seemed as if the most decisive way to beat trouble was to stand alone and meet it head on.

The Wild One

Whether it was on the 4th of July 1947 or sometime in 1950, a short-lived reign of terror by a motorcycle club in a quiet California town grabbed the imagination of filmmaker Stanley Kramer. His 1953 film *The Wild One* starred Marlon Brando and Lee Marvin as two of the violent bikers threatening an insular community. Their uniform and equipment spoke of swift, stinging reprisal as well as rejection of accepted values: the powerful motorbikes (also used by the highway patrol) sounding like giant hornets; the short flight jackets, similar to those worn by World War II pilots and generals as well as U.S. law-enforcement officers, of black leather, and blue jeans, worn with T-shirts.

This was the clothing that became identified in the public's mind with greasers and eventually the Hell's Angels.

The Right Not to Conform

Two more American films were to grab the attention of the young: *On the Waterfront* (1954) and *Rebel Without a Cause* (1955). The first concerned one man's (Brando's) rebellion against authority (in this case, the gangland hold over the docks) and its ruthless exercise of power. Denim jackets, jeans and plaid shirts worn without ties took on a new romance, especially when similar dress was worn by the other great youth hero of the fifties cinema, James Dean.

In *Rebel Without a Cause* James Dean – hair swept up and dressed in jeans, T-shirt and jacket – played a rootless, defiant teenager unable to communicate with his parents, themselves trapped in an unhappy marriage. Not surprisingly, Dean's untimely death, in a road accident in October 1955, turned the actor into an international cult figure.

Rockabilly

A cheap B-movie of 1954 caused a storm both in the United States and Britain. *Blackboard Jungle*'s message of juvenile misbehavior and rowdiness was loathed by adults and loved by teenagers, who felt that Bill Haley's song "Rock around the Clock" summed up their feelings: life is short, let's enjoy it.

As for the audience, the boys sat in the usual adult tailored suit or leisure wear, but with the hair in a slight pompadour and if necessary blacked-in sideburns, while the girls sat in their seats, in pencil-slim skirts and twin sweater sets, or shirt-waisted dresses or full skirts and narrow fitting blouses. Their hair was drawn back in a ponytail or French twist, or framed the face in waves and curls, with their lips glowing with the newest lipstick shades such as "Hound Dog Orange" and "Heartbreak Hotel Pink."

None of that passive enjoyment was for British Teddy Boys.

Teddy Boys

Teddy Boys were first spotted in London's East End in 1952, and by 1956 groups could be seen throughout Britain hanging around streetlamps or jiving and stomping in cinema aisles. The look wasn't cheap, the suit alone could cost three or four weeks' pay. On the feet were suede shoes with thick crepe soles called "brothel creepers," with vivid Day-Glo colored socks. Narrow "drainpipe" trousers (14 inches at the ankle), sometimes with 4-inch cuffs, were worn with a long "finger-tip" single-breasted, drape jacket with a single back vent, sloping padded shoulders and velvet trims. Underneath there was a flashy satin or Lurex waistcoat over a white poplin shirt with a Boston collar, Slim Jim or shoestring tie. A carefully coiffed DA, which received endless attention, and long sideburns were the final touches. The Teddy Boys had no political or moral message for the world. They just liked looking good.

James Dean and friends in jeans,
T-shirts and leather jackets. A still
from *Rebel Without a Cause* (1955).

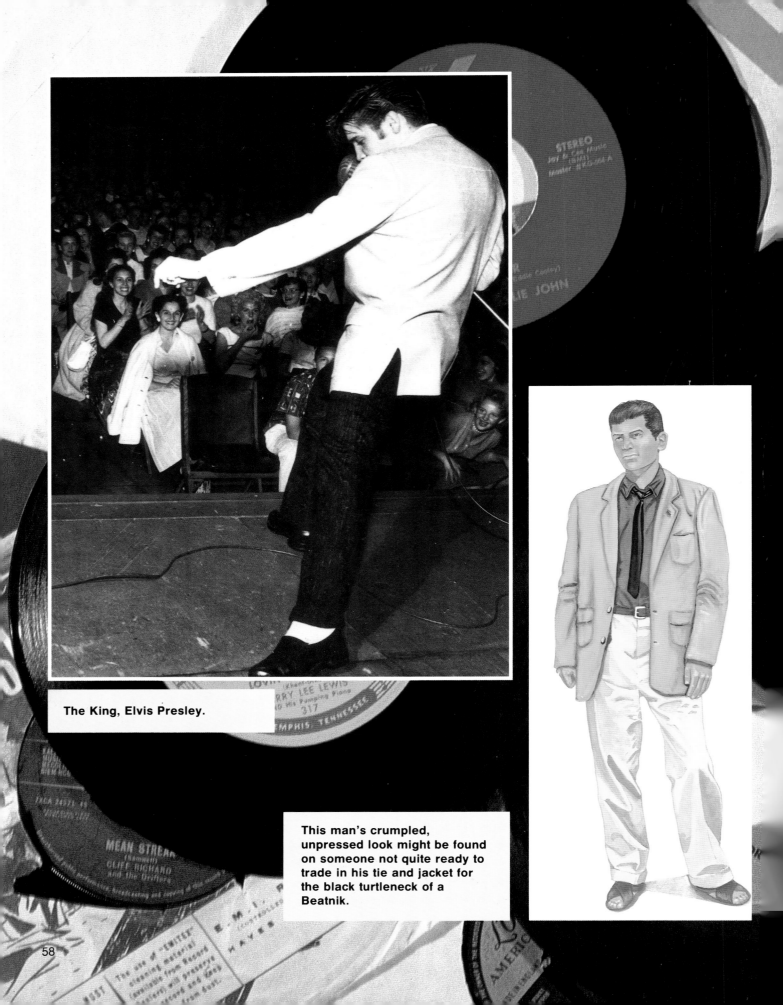

The King, Elvis Presley.

This man's crumpled, unpressed look might be found on someone not quite ready to trade in his tie and jacket for the black turtleneck of a Beatnik.

The British Teddy Boy of the 1950s.

Jerry Lee Lewis using his piano in an unorthodox way.

Glossary

Amies, Hardy (1909–) British born, he became known for his tailored suits and lavish ball-gowns, designing for ladies of the British aristocracy and Royal family.

Balenciaga, Cristobal (1895–1972) By the early 1930s he was Spain's leading fashion designer, but moved to Paris in 1936. With his dramatic designs in strong rich colors, he is believed by many fashion commentators to be the great innovator of the post-war period.

Balmain, Pierre (1914–82) French born, he worked with Molyneux before opening his own salon in 1945. With a reputation for elegant tailoring, he quickly realized the sales potential of boutique accessories and the ready-to-wear market.

Bettina (Bettina Graziani) One of the top Paris models of the fifties, she worked exclusively for Givenchy, who in turn named a full, ruffle-sleeve blouse in *broderie anglaise* after her.

Cardin, Pierre (1922–) Born in Italy, but educated in France, he became an established theatre costume designer before moving into menswear. Having worked for Paquin, Schiaparelli and Dior, he opened a salon in 1950, producing his first collection three years later.

Cashin, Bonnie (1915–) American born, she began by designing for theatre and films before working for sportswear manufacturers. She opened her own New York salon in 1953 and quickly became known for her clean, uncomplicated designs.

Cavanagh, John (1914–) Irish born, he trained in London, Paris and New York before joining Balmain's team in Paris in 1947. He returned to London in 1952 to open his own salon, retiring in 1974.

Chanel, (Gabrielle) Coco (1883–1971) An established French designer, she reopened her salon in 1954 after World War II to a mixed reception, as she rejected the New Look of Dior. However, by the early sixties, her functional designs had won new admirers.

Dior, Christian (1905–57) French designer who had instant success with his first collection, the Corolla line (renamed the New Look), in 1947. He continued to exert great influence on the *haute couture* world until his death in 1957, by which time his salon had expanded into a multi-million dollar fashion business.

Fath, Jacques (1912–54) became established in Paris in 1937 but achieved world-wide fame after World War II for his witty and light touch. One of the first French designers to create for the ready-to-wear market in the early fifties.

Ferragamo, Salvatore (1898–1960) Born in Naples, Italy, he moved to the West Coast of the U.S. in 1914, where he later worked in various film studios. Returning to Italy, he set up a shoe boutique in Florence and by 1957 had created 20,000 styles and registered 350 patents.

Givenchy, Hubert de (1927–) French born, he worked for Fath, Piguet, Lelong and Schiaparelli before establishing his own fashion house. Acknowledged to be the creator of the sack dress, he enjoyed the challenge of designing for films

Hartnell, (Sir) Norman (1901–79) British designer, showing his first collection in Paris in 1927. Appointed dressmaker to the British royal family in 1938, designing both the wedding dress and coronation robes for Princess Elizabeth. Known for his embroidered evening gowns and tailored suits.

Ivy Leaguers Students of East Coast colleges in the 1950s. Men wore neat jackets and pressed trousers with white shirts with a buttoned down collar and tie. Female students dressed in twin sweater sets, or Peter-Pan collared blouses and sweaters, with pencil-slim or pleated skirts.

Jourdan, Charles An established shoe-maker and designer before the Second World War, he opened a Paris boutique in 1957. He was quickly granted the Dior licence to design and manufacture the shoewear for that fashion house.

Mainbocher (Main Rousseau Bocher) (1891–1976) American designer, who worked in London, Munich and Paris. First a fashion artist and journalist, he then became editor of *Vogue* (French edition) and designed for Wallis Simpson, duchess of Windsor, before retiring in 1971. His collection in 1939, before he returned to the USA, anticipated Dior's post-war New Look.

Mattli, Guiseppe (1907–82) Swiss born, he worked in both London and Paris before opening his salon in London in 1934. In 1955, he ceased to design a couture collection.

McCardell, Claire (1905–58) American designer, favoring a functional look in practical fabrics, she is considered to have been one of the USA's most influential designers for the modern career woman.

Norell, Norman (1900–72) American born, he became well known for his Hollywood and Broadway costume designs from the twenties, and his sequin-sheath evening dresses remained a firm favorite among American society circles for many years.

Pucci, Emilio (1914–) A Neapolitan aristocrat by birth, he was educated in the USA. His interest in sports led him to design some winter ski-outfits which caught the attention of the fashion magazine *Harper's Bazaar* (USA). He became *the* fifties sports- and leisure-wear designer.

St. Laurent, Yves (1936–) Born in Algeria, he was employed by Dior in 1953 and took over on Dior's death in 1957, bringing in the Trapeze Line and the "little girl look" to haute couture the following year.

Stiebel, Victor (1907–76) Born in South Africa, he first set up his salon in London in 1932, which closed at the outbreak of war. He reopened in 1952 and became a favorite designer for fashionable outfits for Ascot and other British horse races.

Reading List

A great deal has been written and published about the nineteen fifties – this reading list is only a very small selection. Magazines and movies of the period are another excellent source of information.

Adult General Reference Sources

Calasibetta, Charlotte, *Essential Terms of Fashion: A Collection of Definitions* (Fairchild, 1985).
Calasibetta, Charlotte, *Fairchild's Dictionary of Fashion,* 2nd Edition (Fairchild, 1988).
Gold, Annalee, *90 Years of Fashion* (Fairchild, 1990).
O'Hara, Georgina, *The Encyclopedia of Fashion* (Harry N. Abrams, 1986).
Trahey, Jane (Ed.), *100 Years of the American Female From Harper's Bazaar* (Random House, 1967).

Young Adult Sources

Ruby, Jennifer, *The Nineteen Forties & Nineteen Fifties*, "Costume in Context" series (David & Charles, 1989).
Wilcox, R. Turner, *Five Centuries of American Costume* (Scribner's, 1963).

Acknowledgments

The author and publishers would like to thank the following for permission to reproduce illustrations: AP/Wide World Photos for page 58; BFI Stills for pages 3, 14, 16, 29, 33, 48, 50a, 51a, 54a, 55, 57; The Hulton Picture Company for pages 9, 13, 21, 24, 25a, 31, 41, 45, 52, 56; International Wool Secretariat for page 25b; The Kobal Collection for pages 15 and 49; Lighthorne Pictures for pages 8, 11, 23, 28, 30a, 32, 63; Lighthorne Pictures/Naked City Pictures for pages 58–59; Popperfoto for pages 6, 26–27, 30b, 40, 42a; Publisher's Collection for pages 17, 44 and 46a; Rex Features for pages 12 and 59; The Vintage Magazine Co. for pages 7, 10, 18, 19, 20, 22, 34a, 35, 36a, 37, 42a, 46b. The illustrations were researched by David Pratt.

Time Chart

NEWS	EVENTS	FASHIONS
50 War in Korea President Truman confirms H-bomb program.	Introduction of the credit card system in USA. First ever mass-production of computers.	Paris decrees that hemlines are 16 inches off the ground. Emilio Pucci opens his fashion house.
51 Juan Peron reelected president of Argentina.	The rock and roll era begins. First color TV broadcasts in USA.	Balmain opens his ready-to-wear boutique in New York City. Balenciaga shows a waistless dress in his autumn collection.
52 Dwight Eisenhower becomes president of the United States.	Teddy Boys are sighted in London's East End.	End of British clothes rationing. Cavanagh and Stiebel open salons in London. Givenchy shows his first collection.
53 Coronation of Queen Elizabeth II. Death of Stalin. McCarthy Senate hearings open. Official end to segregration in U.S. military.	Mount Everest is climbed for the first time. James Baldwin publishes *Go Tell It on the Mountain*.	Bonnie Cashin opens her New York salon.
54 French forces defeated at Dien Bien Phu. The end of French power in Vietnam.	1 person in 7 has a TV set in the USA, contrasted to 1 in 24 in Britain. Bill Haley appears in *Black-Board Jungle*.	Coco Chanel reopens her Paris fashion house. Fath dies.
55 Civil rights movements begins with Montgomery bus boycott.	Sloane Wilson publishes his novel *Man in the Gray Flannel Suit*. James Dean dies in road accident.	Mary Quant opens her boutique in London, with clothes aimed at those under-25.
56 The Suez crisis.	Elvis Presley arrives as an international star with the hit "Heartbreak Hotel."	First major Italian fashion show in New York.
57 Demonstrations in Little Rock, Arkansas. Sputnik I in orbit.	First meeting of the Channel Tunnel Company in Britain. *West Side Story* opens on the New York stage.	In Paris, Dior is the only designer to show a waistline in his collection. He dies soon after. Givenchy shows the Sack.
58 Charles de Gaulle becomes French president.	Wedding of Arthur Miller and Marilyn Monroe. Elvis Presley is drafted into the U.S. Army.	Yves St. Laurent introduces the Trapeze Line. Paris decrees that hems are above the knee.
59 Castro overthrows the Batista regime in Cuba.	The synthesizer appears as a new musical instrument.	St. Laurent revives the hobble skirt for the House of Dior. Suits from Mary Quant prefigure the styles of the 1960s.

Bronwen Pugh, one of the famous Paris fashion faces of the fifties. Her looks are typical of the cool, elegant, even haughty-looking models favored by photographers and designers at the time.

Index

Numbers in *italics* refer to illustrations.